Original title:
Peach Skies and Summer Nights

Copyright © 2025 Creative Arts Management OÜ
All rights reserved.

Author: Fiona Harrington
ISBN HARDBACK: 978-1-80586-406-6
ISBN PAPERBACK: 978-1-80586-878-1

Laughter in the Warmth

Beneath the glow of waning light,
We chase the shadows out of sight.
A kite got stuck in Grandma's hair,
She laughed so hard, she lost her chair.

Ice cream drips on noses bright,
Squirrels steal our snacks in flight.
We stumble, tumble, dance with glee,
For summer's laugh sets spirits free.

Horizon's Gentle Caress

The sun bows down, a comedy,
As flip-flops fly in revelry.
With every breeze a giggle gained,
As birds tease our hair, unrestrained.

The grass becomes a stage tonight,
With crickets playing songs of light.
A dog joins in the silly fray,
As laughter sprawls and waltzes play.

Warmth Wrapped in Color

In fields where daisies make their stand,
We paint our dreams with ice cream sand.
Our frisbee's soaring, but wait—what's that?
A squirrel's now in the batting hat!

The sun throws gold from high above,
While ants march on, so full of love.
A watermelon fight ensues,
And laughter echoes, bright and hues.

Serenade of the Fireflies

Fireflies flicker like our eyes,
As we tell tales beneath the skies.
The glow brings giggles, sparkles bright,
Each wrong punchline ignites delight.

With marshmallows roasted to a beat,
We dance around, feel brave and fleet.
A rumor spreads: the moon has a hat,
And laughter rolls like a friendly cat.

Solstice Night's Tender Kiss

The fireflies dance with crazy flair,
Their twinkling lights fill the warm night air.
A cat in a hat thinks he's a dog,
Stealing a seat on the porch's log.

With lemonade spills and ice cream fights,
We laugh 'til we cry under soft starlights.
A neighbor's BBQ turns into a fling,
As burgers mysteriously sprout tiny wings.

Where Shadows Play in Gold

The sun dips low, a swirly show,
In flip-flops, we giggle, dancing slow.
A squirrel in shades gives us a grin,
As we try to catch the breeze on a whim.

We race the clouds, though we're out of breath,
Chasing the wind like it's a pet.
The ice cream truck plays a silly tune,
While a puppy tries to howl at the moon.

Moments Wrapped in Warmth

A picnic basket spills out, oh no!
Sandwiches fly like a breaded show.
Ants plot a coup for a juicy slice,
While we argue 'bout which game is nice.

The night wraps us like a cozy hug,
As marshmallows roast in a gooey mug.
A dance-off starts with a wobbling flair,
While grandma gets stuck in a lawn chair.

Horizons Blushing with Promises

The horizon blushes, oh what a sight,
A sea of red and orange delight.
A seagull steals fries from a clueless chap,
While everyone laughs and points at the flap.

The breeze can't help but tease our hair,
A kite gets tangled without a care.
As laughter echoes, the stars peek through,
We cherish these moments, wild and true.

Serendipity of Creamy Skies

In a land of fluff and joy,
Pigs fly high, folks shout ahoy!
Ice cream drips down little Becca,
She swears it's just a sticky Mecca.

Lizards dance in neon light,
Giggling kids take flight at night.
Every swing is a banana boat,
With frosting waves, we'll surely float.

Squirrels steal a pizza slice,
Chasing birds, they roll like dice.
On this funny, dreamy quest,
Nothing's weird, it's all the best!

Even clouds wear silly hats,
While kittens play and chase their mats.
In this land of funky charms,
Nothing's safe from magic's arms!

Tranquility at the Edge of Night

Fireflies twinkle like stars in jeans,
While cats plot schemes with funny means.
Waffles sing a sleepy song,
As owls hoot, 'Don't take too long!'

Bubbly dreams float on moonbeams,
While marshmallow clouds sail in teams.
A raccoon dance-off on the lawn,
Critters party till the dawn!

Giant cookies smile and bake,
Bold cupcakes giggle as they wake.
With sprinkles flying everywhere,
It's a treat without a care!

Laughter rules the velvet breeze,
Leaves rumble down like happy tease.
In this night, so wild and bright,
We're all stars in this delight!

Lanterns in the Velvet Dark

Jellybeans glow in lustrous hues,
As llamas dance in funky shoes.
Marshmallow fires light up the trees,
Balloons collide with buzzing bees.

Moonlit paths hold trails of glee,
Where unicorns sip tepid tea.
Ghosts in tutus pirouette,
With every chuckle, no regret.

Lanterns flicker, spill their cheer,
While bouncing pies flip through the air.
Silly shadows dance and play,
Turning nighttime into a parade!

As laughter echoes, hearts unite,
In wondrous joy, we scurry light.
Each funny moment finds a spark,
Brightening up the velvet dark!

Soft Shadows and Sweet Memories

In the backyard, we run with glee,
Chasing fireflies, just you and me.
The dog steals the sandwich from my hand,
While we laugh, like it's all unplanned.

Mom's lemonade spills on my brand new shirt,
I trip on the grass, oh how it hurt!
We giggle at life, and all its quirks,
Under the sun, where mischief lurks.

Sultry Breezes and Stardust

The breeze whispers secrets, oh so sly,
As I toss water balloons, oh my!
My cousin dodges, but slips on the slide,
And we laugh so hard, we can't hide.

Popcorn kernels fly like confetti in the air,
Sticky fingers pointing, laughter to share.
We craft our dreams with giggles and sighs,
While mischief dances beneath evening skies.

A Dance of Light and Shadow

In the garden, we make forts of leaves,
Sneaking snacks, oh how it deceives!
A squirrel steals the last chip I had,
Watching it frolic, it's just too bad.

One cat sprawls, claiming my sunlit space,
While we plot our escape from this place.
With goofy faces, we mimic the birds,
Creating a symphony of silly words.

Sunkissed Echoes

As the sun dips low, we dance in shadows,
Silly pirouettes, oh how it grows!
We drop ice cream cones, and then we scream,
Painting our night with a wild dream.

A twinkling star falls, a wish to make,
I wish for more laughter, and less heartache.
But instead, we find worms in our cake,
And laugh at the silly, the great big mistake.

Nostalgia in the Air

Ice cream drips down to my toes,
While my dog chases all the crows.
Laughter bubbles like fizzy drinks,
Silly hats are what everyone thinks.

Shorts too bright, like a summer's ray,
With mismatched socks, I dance and sway.
Friends on swings, we laugh and shout,
What's that smell? Is it burnt-out clout?

Harmonies of Warm Evenings

Fireflies buzz like tiny stars,
Jokes exchanged without any bars.
S'mores stuck in my hair so sweet,
Sticky fingers and dancing feet.

Cicadas chirp a funny tune,
While the moon laughs at our cartoon.
Hot dogs dropped, some ketchup's flung,
We giggle loud, forever young.

Comfort of a Firelit Dusk

Crickets serenade a silly joke,
S'mores are melting, we're all bespoke.
Tales of ghosts that aren't in sight,
But my friend shrieks with all his might.

Marshmallows jumping, oh what a sight,
Bugs crash parties, but we'll be right.
Fires crackle, sparkles soar,
Laughter loud, can't ask for more.

Secrets Carried by the Wind

Whispers swirl on a soft breeze,
Tickling noses like teasing bees.
Popsicle stains on my favorite shirt,
Wishing the grass would stop being hurt.

Bicycles squeak down the sunlit lane,
Laughter dances through joy and pain.
Giggling secrets, plans to concoct,
While the neighborhood's hilariously shocked.

Vows Underneath Lavender Skies

We stood beneath the twilight's gaze,
Promised love in silly ways.
A cake of frogs, a dance of glee,
My socks were lost, but who cares, see?

Serenade the moonlight bright,
With twirling moves, we took flight.
The neighbors peeked, they laughed aloud,
While we forgot we were quite proud.

I vowed to share my snack with you,
A roll of cheese, or maybe two.
You swore to wear my goofy hat,
As long as you'd bring the snacks to chat.

So here we are, two jolly fools,
With laughter ringing like old school rules.
In lavender hues, we call it fate,
Our vows in giggles, oh, how great!

A Night Touched by Magic

They said the stars would dance and play,
But really, they just looked our way.
A wand made from a breadstick long,
I waved it, and it felt so wrong.

We summoned treats from thin air,
Popcorn clouds and laughter share.
A potion brewed in Grandma's mug,
Spilled jelly beans—a sticky hug.

The moon was caught in a feathery thrill,
Dreaming of dancing on a hill.
With giggles erupting like summer rain,
We chased the fireflies, feeling no pain.

Oh, magic laughed like silly dreams,
While we danced in rainbow beams.
A night so wild, it felt so right,
With just a splash of nonsense delight!

Murmurs of the Night Air

Whispers float on velvet breeze,
Bugs are singing, if you please.
A cat in shades, a crow with flair,
Pull a joker from thin air!

We chase the giggles through the dark,
Stealing laughter, what a lark!
The world feels full of winks and nods,
As we dance beside the sleeping gods.

A trumpet made of tangled weeds,
Plays the song of summer's needs.
Spinning tales of jest and cheer,
While crickets tune their music near.

In murmurs soft, we rule the night,
Trading dreams for silly flight.
It's a realm where shadows play,
Enticing joy to lead the way!

Nostalgic Radiance

Remember when we shared that fall?
Giggling like children, feeling so small.
A lemonade fountain, taste of delight,
With friends who danced like silly sprites.

The road was paved with our bright schemes,
We chased the sun and lived our dreams.
Donuts stolen from a distant shop,
Each bite a dive—a sugary plop!

A sunset stained with rainbow flare,
We mocked the clouds, tossed away care.
Our laughter echoed through the trees,
To summon joy with playful ease.

In golden hues of our playful past,
We hold the moments, wanting them to last.
With nostalgic radiance lighting our way,
We weave our follies into a bright ballet!

Lightly Leaden Skies

Balloons afloat, escape our hands,
We chase them down, like hungry bands.
A squirrel stole my sandwich, oh what a sight,
I'm left with crumbs and a noble plight.

The ice cream drips, and so do my pants,
I laugh it off and attempt a dance.
The sun says goodbye in a comical flair,
As ants march on, like they don't care.

Evening's Gentle Revelry

Fireflies flicker, a dinner guest,
They twinkle around, putting me to the test.
I wave my arms, they tease and retreat,
Like a game of tag with my own two feet.

Picnic blankets turned upside down,
Sandwiches flying like they wear a crown.
A breeze whispers secrets, what could it be?
The neighbor's cat just stole my sweet tea.

Starlit Reverberations

The moon's in a mood, glowing pale blue,
Like it's had too much party, who even knew?
We dance on the grass with multiple flair,
Tripping over shadows as we gasp for air.

Laughter erupts, and so does a sprout,
Curtains of laughter, not a single doubt.
We take selfies with friends, but alas, oh dear,
The camera's just frozen, it captures a cheer.

Charcoal Hues of Dusk

The sun dips low, painting mischief anew,
Kites tangle in trees, oh what a view!
Lemonade spills like it's trying to escape,
While we giggle softly, in our summer cape.

The grill's on fire, well not in a way,
That's edible, juicy, what more can I say?
The evening unfolds with a funny little twist,
As my cousin trips, I can't resist the list!

Golden Hour Reveries

The sun dips low, oh what a sight,
Tommy found a kite that took flight.
It tangled in a tree's embrace,
And now it's waving with such grace.

We laughed and chased, oh what a chase,
As bugs flew by, some hit my face.
Ice cream dripped on my new shirt,
I guess that's how summer can hurt!

Dreams Beneath the Evening Glow

The fireflies danced like tiny stars,
I thought of all my dream-filled jars.
But crashed a party with my loud snores,
I think they left, slamming their doors.

We sat on logs, telling bad jokes,
While the raccoons robbed us like crooks.
I wondered why the moon looked shy,
Maybe it's hiding from our pie.

Soft Breezes and Starry Visions

The breeze came in, a playful tease,
Knocking off hats with such great ease.
I chased mine down, but it was a race,
While laughing birds mocked my disgrace.

We shared cold drinks with funny straws,
Pretended we were on a cruise, just because.
But then I spilled it on my friend,
Now he smells like cola till summer's end!

Dusk's Embrace

The grill was hot, but so was I,
I flipped the burgers, tried not to fry.
One flew off and landed near a pup,
He looked bewildered as I yelled, "Stop!"

Beneath the stars, we made a wish,
For all our troubles, what a dish!
But who knew wishes could bring such glee,
When my brother tripped and fell on me!

Where Time Melts and Glows

Chasing ice cream trucks with glee,
Their jingle's a symphony, don't you see?
Neighbors wave with popsicles in hand,
While squirrels plot a nutty heist, oh so grand.

Lawn chairs creak like old guitars,
As kids craft rockets from candy bars.
The sun winks as it dips low,
While ants steal crumbs like they're in a show.

Jokes fly like paper planes on the breeze,
We laugh 'til our sides are sore, oh please!
Fireflies dance in the twilight's glow,
Claiming the backyard like they're in a show.

Bubbles float softly, like secrets shared,
And laughter echoes, as if it dared.
With every sip of lemonade served,
We toast to moments hugely preserved.

Tapestry of Warm Nights

The neighbors' cat patrols the fence,
Looking regal, but he's just pretentious.
A game of tag breaks out with cheers,
While shadows stretch and count the years.

Picnic blankets sprinkled around,
With crumbs of laughter all over the ground.
A watermelon seed-spitting contest,
Declares the champion wildly blessed.

Chasing rhymes in a flickering light,
We recite bad jokes, oh what a sight!
Stars pop up, like they're in on the fun,
As we guffaw, beneath the golden sun.

A dog barks loud, trying to sing,
Not quite in tune; oh, the joy it brings!
Neighbors peep out, with a grin, not a frown,
At our parade of laughter, we wear it like a crown.

Serenades of the Sinking Sun

The grill sizzles like a summer song,
As burgers flip, where memories belong.
A cat takes a nap right on your plate,
Claiming the food like it's a grand estate.

Kids concoct tales of dragon fights,
With cardboard shields into starry nights.
A frisbee flies, then it smacks a tree,
Leaving behind giggles, wild and free.

Mismatched chairs all in a row,
Wobbly and silly, but they steal the show.
The laughter rises with chilly drinks,
While sparklers crackle, and no one thinks.

Finally, smores melt in delight,
As marshmallows bounce into the night.
With goofy grins and sweet sticky hands,
We savor the magic that summer commands.

Embraces Under the Orange Horizon

Twilight curls like a dog on the floor,
As laughter erupts at every door.
A bicycle race, with helmets askew,
And someone falls, but they're laughing too.

Glow sticks wiggle, like excited worms,
As kids try to capture the evening terms.
A bug parade marches to the beat,
While sandals slip off tiny feet.

Pizza rolls bounce on a makeshift throne,
While someone's dance moves are overblown.
Neighbors peek out, with popcorn in hand,
As we boogie down on the patio land.

The day waves goodbye with a silly wink,
And it's time to toast with a cold drink.
With giggles and stories, we'll gather near,
Embracing the sunset, filled with cheer.

Golden Hues and Dusk's Embrace

The sun drops low, the dogs all bark,
We try to catch fireflies in the dark.
Chasing shadows and laughing loud,
While neighbors wonder what makes us proud.

The kids are sticky with melting treats,
Ice cream drips down, and chaos repeats.
We trip over chairs in a silly race,
Trying to dodge the sprinkler's spray.

Clouds blush pink like cotton candy dreams,
As we plot our escape to the ice cream seams.
Frogs serenade us with their silly croaks,
While dad pulls puns that make us choke.

We lie on grass, watch stars appear,
Swapping ghost stories, and stifling fear.
With every burst of laughter shared,
We forget the world, with no one else cared.

Whispering Breezes at Twilight

The wind whispers secrets, oh so sly,
As we concoct tales of dragons that fly.
Our bikes tumble down like fallen leaves,
While we plan to build forts on the eaves.

Jumping in puddles, we splash and squeal,
Mischief is brewing with every meal.
A dog with a sock, what a scenic sight,
He's led another poor chase, just for spite.

Fireside tales of the great and bold,
Mixed with marshmallows that scorch, then fold.
We laugh through the acrid scent of smoke,
While grandpa insists he'll teach us a joke.

Swapping stories till the moon is high,
Imagining aliens zooming by.
Our joyful chaos a delightful sound,
As dusk turns to mischief, all around.

A Canvas of Warmth

The sky's a canvas of silly flair,
With crayons mounting a colorful dare.
We paint with giggles and fruity spills,
Creating wind chimes from berry peels.

A towel kingdom draped on the grass,
With a throne made from cushions, set to amass.
The ruler of berries, too juicy to save,
Commands the minions, we line up like brave.

Squirrels join in for the banquet feast,
While ants wage war, no one claimed the least.
We trade our snacks, each bite a jackpot,
As if chocolate chips are a treasure lot.

In this warm cocoon where laughter swells,
We hide from the world, with its toils and spells.
Our banquet of nonsense, a feast for the soul,
While the evening air wraps around like a shoal.

Dreams in the Gentle Glow

The glow from the stars is just like a joke,
We laugh too hard till a soda chokes.
Bedtime's a elusion, as giggles persist,
Trading loud whispers, oh what a twist!

Pillows become castles, with knights so grand,
While critters outside throw a wild band.
Our dreams float in freely, refusing to pause,
Under the vigil of firefly laws.

With leftover snacks and wild debates,
Mighty adventures on imaginary plates.
Fortune cookies crack with a silly sound,
As we plot to sneak snacks we swore would be bound.

Then drift off into slumber late in the night,
As moonbeams hustle, bringing dreams alive bright.
In a realm of laughter, and mischief we find,
The gentle glow keeps our spirits entwined.

Coastal Twilight

The sun dips low, a clown in retreat,
Seagulls squawk jokes, they can't be beat.
Sandcastles crumble, oh what a sight,
Waves laughing hard, in the fading light.

Jellyfish dance, a wobbly show,
Crabs shuffle by with a comical glow.
Shells sing tunes of lost beach ball dreams,
While kids play tag in their ice cream schemes.

Bright umbrellas bob like silly hats,
Piña coladas sent through seagull chats.
The day winds down, with a splash and a cheer,
As flip-flops flop, bringing laughter near.

Melodies of the Warm Evening

Fireflies blink like a disco ball,
Crickets play symphonies, a caterwaul.
A raccoon rummages, looking for pies,
While the moon grins down with slanted eyes.

The barbecue sizzles, the steaks have a chat,
"Don't burn me, buddy, I'm not a brat!"
Friends crack jokes in the smoky haze,
As shadows twist in a whimsical craze.

Marshmallows tumble, a gooey delight,
S'mores in hand, it's a sugary fight.
Laughter erupts as one takes a fall,
Summer's sweet songtime will beckon us all.

Flickering Flames and Hidden Secrets

The campfire pops with a magical spark,
Ghost stories told, while the dogs bark.
S'mores are made with a wobbly hand,
Sticky fingers, oh isn't life grand?

Whispers float like marshmallows high,
In the cool night air, secrets do fly.
Everyone's trying to roast the first treat,
But they char them all, now that's quite a feat!

Laughter erupts, a truly grand time,
Someone's told a joke — it doesn't quite rhyme.
As the stars twinkle, and sparks rise up,
We sip from our cups like a hiccuping cup.

Celestial Strokes of Pastel

Cotton candy clouds in crazy hues,
Kids make wishes on their shiny shoes.
The sky is a canvas, splashed with bliss,
And gravity seems just a hit or miss.

A hot air balloon drifts like a dream,
While dogs chase bubbles in a sunbeam.
Picnics laid out like a feast in a park,
Squirrels conspire, plotting their spark.

The breeze tells riddles, with giggles and glee,
As ice cream drips just as fast as can be.
With sun-kissed faces, life's one big laugh,
We dance in the shade, like a joyful giraffe.

Mellow Melodies and Magic

A cat in a hat dances through the grass,
Chasing its tail while the minutes pass.
The ice cream truck jingles, oh what a sight,
As squirrels conspire to steal a delight.

Jumping in puddles, oh what a splash!
A summer's day turns into a bash.
With lemonade smiles and cookies galore,
Who knew the garden could be such a roar?

The sun winks softly, all golden and bright,
While fireworks giggle and burst in the night.
A frog on a lily in shades of green,
Turns out to be the best friend you've seen.

So let's twirl like silly in this joyful spree,
With laughter and nonsense, just you and me.
In a world where the wild things take flight,
We'll dance with the shadows and shout with delight.

Soft Serenades of the Night

Beneath a blanket, the stars are aglow,
With marshmallow dreams that float like a show.
A raccoon with flair comes to join in our fun,
Hoping to trade us a biscuit for a pun.

Fireflies twinkle like grand little sprites,
While we roast the best of our ghostly bites.
With stories of dragons that tickle your ear,
And monsters that dance, ensuring good cheer.

The moon plays the banjo, with crickets in stride,
As laughter erupts from a hedge full of pride.
In this quirky universe, joy takes its flight,
Where shadows turn silly and giggles ignite.

So here's to the magic that sprinkles tonight,
In a world that can turn every wrong into right.
With friends made of sugar and hearts made of glee,
We'll fill the warm air with our wild, happy spree.

Euphoria Beneath Starry Canopies

Under the twinkle of fairy light dreams,
A penguin with shades slides down ice creams.
While owls in tuxedos sip tea with a grin,
We frolic with gnomes that play violin.

The grass plays a tune as we chase after cheese,
A picnic of laughter carried on the breeze.
An octopus juggles, impressive display,
While squirrels hold acorns in a cheeky ballet.

Across the horizon, the sun wiggles low,
With splashes of orange in a comical show.
A flamingo struts by, all feathers and flair,
As we laugh off our worries because who needs despair?

So here's to the magic, a world of delight,
Where every odd moment makes everything right.
With joy as our compass, we dance through the glow,
In a festival of whimsy, let happiness grow.

Hues of a Gentle Goodbye

As day turns to night, the sun takes a dip,
A turtle named Timmy does a silly flip.
With giggles ablaze, we watch shadows play,
The light in the distance slowly fades away.

A llama in shades gives a wink and a wave,
While night serenades in a croaky, sweet bray.
The fire burns low, toasting marshmallows bright,
With chocolatey smiles, we relish the night.

A breeze starts to dance, whispering secrets untold,
As whimsy entwines with the warmth of the bold.
With hugs and high-fives and a wink of the eye,
We'll cherish this moment, a sweet little goodbye.

So let laughter linger, like stars in the sky,
In this joyful adventure, you and I.
With memories painted in colors that gleam,
We'll treasure these minutes, forever we'll dream.

Evening's Sanguine Song

The sun dips low with a grin,
As fireflies start to play,
A raccoon struts with a flair,
Thinking he's here to stay.

Laughter echoes from the park,
Kids chase shadows and laughs,
Ice cream drips down a cone,
As joy fills up the drafts.

A picnic blanket's a ship,
Set sail on blanket seas,
With ants as our crewmates,
As we munch on our cheese.

In this twilight, all feels light,
With silly songs and cheer,
We dance like nobody cares,
Though we might spill our beer.

A Tapestry of Distant Dreams

The moon peeks out with a wink,
As stars begin to chatter,
We toss our cares in the air,
Like confetti made of batter.

Cats in hats march in style,
On fences made for kings,
While neighbors shake their heads,
At our improvised swing flings.

A soft breeze tickles our cheeks,
And laughter paints the night,
Each giggle like a firework,
Igniting pure delight.

So let's toast to all the dreams,
That dance upon the grass,
With twinkling eyes and full plates,
Wishing all moments last.

Flickers of Longing

As dusk wraps around us tight,
We share stories and fries,
The toast is burnt but it's fine,
And no one seems to mind.

A squirrel steals the last chip,
With a plan all in his head,
We cheer him on with delight,
While crumbs fall from our bread.

Bubbles float like dreams on air,
As childhood echoes near,
We chase them down with wild glee,
While giggling without fear.

This moment hangs like ripe fruit,
Just waiting to be plucked,
With laughter tangled in our hair,
We know we're truly lucked.

Day's Farewell

The sun waves bye with a cheer,
As sky coats itself in peach,
We spot a cow on a roof,
Wondering how it got there to preach.

Chasing shadows of the past,
While dogs try to catch their tails,
Each bark a lighthearted tune,
In a night of silly trails.

As lights begin to pop and twinkle,
The crickets burst into song,
With a dance of happy feet,
We know we all belong.

So raise a glass to memories,
To laughter and to cheer,
In the cozy arms of twilight,
Where joy is ever near.

Secrets of the Sunset

The sun makes a wink, oh what a sight,
As I race my shadow in fading light.
It slips on a banana, falls with a shout,
Leaving me giggling, I leap and pout.

Light snacks for the crickets, a feast they prepare,
As I try to juggle with underwear.
My friends think I'm magic, but they don't know,
It's really just clumsy, putting on a show.

Butterflies laugh at my tripping plight,
Even squirrels join in with pure delight.
As the sky dresses pink, orange, and blue,
We toast with our drinks — oh, don't spill it, too!

The sun takes a bow, an artist in flight,
Leaves us all chuckling, such silly delight.
Rotating on swings, we sing out the tune,
That sunset secrets are best shared with the moon.

Evening's Sweet Serenade

The dusk hums a tune like a bee's busy buzz,
Tickling the air as it softly does.
I dance like a jellybean, fluffy and round,
While the stars poke fun from their faraway ground.

With fireflies glowing like flickering lights,
I try to catch them, oh what silly sights!
They're quick little ninjas, just out of reach,
As I shout, 'Hey! Help me!' to a nearby peach.

The moon gives a glance, with a twinkly smile,
Encouraging me to embrace my style.
A serenade slips through the giggles of glee,
Here's to the chorus of creatures and me!

Even the breeze joins, with a gentle sway,
As I slip on the grass, and the laughter won't stay.
In this melody, joyous, we bask in delight,
Painting our stories on the canvas of night.

Laughter Beneath Open Vistas

Underneath the carnival glow of the sky,
We chase silly dreams with a hop and a sigh.
Kites get tangled, making knots like my hair,
While I pretend I'm a wizard — fairy dust in the air.

A picnic blanket's a throne, I declare,
Where sandwiches giggle and my juice combs the hair.
Friends share their stories, each funnier than last,
While I ride my bike, over the grass, oh so fast!

The breeze whispers jokes only flowers can tell,
As I slip down a hill, oh, I laugh and I yell!
The sunset applauds my trickster parade,
As the sky paints in colors a fine escapade.

With nature as audience, we bow to the night,
In this wacky theater of giggles and light.
The stars take the stage, in their shimmering flight,
As we plot more mischief beneath cosmic sight.

Twilight's Lush Reverie

As twilight unfolds with a giggly cheer,
We stretch out our limbs, chasing shadows near.
Marshmallows are flying, caught in hairdos,
While friends wheeze with laughter, sharing old news.

Grasshoppers croak in a rhythmic ballet,
As I try to leapskip — then stumble and sway.
My ice cream's a mountain, yet I get no bite,
Because it's sliding faster than I can write!

Beneath twinkling stars, our antics unfold,
Each secret unveiled, a new story told.
A breeze carries chuckles from people nearby,
As we plot to prank the moon, oh so shy.

In this lush reverie of giggly delight,
We dance with the twilight, embracing the night.
In the mirth of the moment, we weave and we spin,
Celebrating the joy that lives deep within.

When Daydreams Meet Nightfall

The sun is a jester, painting things bright,
As I chase my pet cat, who's taking flight.
With a bump and a jump, she races away,
While I trip on my shoelace, oh what a day!

Clouds sport their pjs, all fluffy and neat,
While ants throw a party, dancing on feet.
A squirrel in a tux, stealing my snack,
Laughing, I wonder what's next in this whack!

The crickets start crooning their nighttime song,
But here comes my dog, barking all night long.
I reel him in gently, with a pat and a cheer,
And whisper to hope that my neighbors don't hear.

As dusk takes its bow, the stars start to yawn,
The moon's in a hurry, quickly drawn on.
I sit on the porch, a drink in my hand,
With laughter and giggles, isn't life just grand?

Day's Farewell, Night's Arrival

The sun throws confetti, it's time to unwind,
With all of my gadgets left far behind.
The world has gone silly, with laughter and cheer,
As shadows do tango, it's time to adhere.

I spy a lone firefly, trying to glow,
But he's joined by his buddies, and they put on a show.
They bump and they buzz, doing the cha-cha,
While I wave my arms, dancing with a piñata.

The day's been a circus, a whirlwind of fun,
And now comes the night, with a wink and a pun.
The moon's wearing shades, looking cool as it glides,
While owls hoot at jokes, so cleverly hides.

I laugh at the stars, they're twinkling with glee,
As crickets gossip about what they see.
The world slows its pace, with a murmur and clap,
As night wraps its arms around my sunset nap.

Sunset Hues

With colors exploding, the day's dressed to thrill,
Chasing shadows and giggles, we're hanging on still.
The ice cream is melting, drips down my new shirt,
And I'm laughing so hard—yes, I'm really a jerk!

As sunbeams play hide and seek in the trees,
My friends launch a water balloon, aiming with ease.
It lands on my head, oh what a wet sight,
But with laughter we join in the splash fight tonight!

Oranges, pinks, yellows—such a glorious fuss,
As we strut like we own it, riding the bus.
With headbands of flowers, and sun hats askew,
The world's just a stage, with us in the view.

As the sky blushes deep, and the stars start to prance,
We break out the snacks, throw caution to chance.
Because life's just a sketch, we laugh and we play,
Painting joy in the dusk, before night steals the day.

Twilight Whispers

The twilight is giggling, sneaking in fast,
With shadows all dancing, I think I just passed.
A raccoon in a hat is stealing my fries,
I'm sure he's auditioning for late-night disguise!

The crickets are gossiping, floating on air,
A squirrel joins in, with a nut to compare.
As laughter erupts, with my friends by my side,
We're plotting the pranks that we'll never abide.

The first stars peep out, with a wink and a grin,
As I trip over sneakers left carelessly in.
The moon, like a spotlight, brightens the scene,
While the fireflies flicker with lanterns so keen.

The laughter keeps echoing, filling the night,
With friends who ignite every moment with light.
In whispers and secrets, we vow to unite,
Through antics and fun, till morning's first bite.

Midsummer's Color Palette

Sunshine spills like paint on grass,
A frog jumps high, doesn't care for class.
Picnic ants march in a tight parade,
While we debate the best lemonade.

The splash of a hose becomes the new game,
Catching a cloud, oh what a shame!
Ice cream cones melt, sticky and slow,
We laugh as it drips down our toes.

A kite flies high with a silly grin,
Caught in a tree, oh, it's a win-win!
A squirrel steals a sandwich, bold as brass,
While we chase him, rolling on the grass.

Sunset paints the sky in silly hues,
As we chase fireflies and dodge our snooze.
The stars peek out, all twinkly and bright,
As we giggle and plan for the next night.

Whispering Clouds at Dusk

Fluffy whispers float like dreams untold,
As we swap stories both brave and bold.
A raccoon shows off his juggling skills,
We laugh till our stomachs have their fills.

Bubbles sail high, drifting in jest,
A wobbly dance, they never rest.
Two kids chase them, don't trip on a shoe,
While mom sips tea, saying, 'Oh, adieu!'

The sun takes a bow behind the trees,
Crickets join in with a buzzing tease.
A lollipop stick is the sword of choice,
As we combat our imaginary voice.

With sticky fingers and sleepy sighs,
Fireflies twinkle like little spies.
The day waves goodbye with a cheeky grin,
As we plan our mischief for the night to begin.

Embracing the Fading Light

Shadows stretch out like they're playing tag,
Chasing after the sun, a cheerful wag.
Fire pits crackle as s'mores get made,
But we're just here for the marshmallow trade.

Old chairs squeak, they tell their own tales,
While we spin stories like daring sails.
The moon peeks out, with a wink and a nod,
As we argue over who played the best odd.

Bikes race down paths, tires squealing in glee,
A watermelon slice as our referee.
Laughter erupts as a slip and a fall,
We jump back up, like it's not a big haul.

The fireflies compete with the stars for fame,
As we gather around to chant our own names.
The day melts away like ice on a spoon,
And we plan for tomorrow under a bright moon.

Evening Drifts on Lavender Winds

In twilight's embrace, we float like the breeze,
A dog chases shadows, oh what a tease!
We hop over puddles, trying not to slip,
Laughing so hard that we start to trip.

Cicadas serenade with a buzzing tune,
As we play hide and seek with the moon.
Sneaky little stars join the fray,
Winking at secrets that vanish in play.

A cat in a hat joins our merry crew,
Strutting like royalty, what will he do?
Twinkling laughter fills the nighttime air,
While we ponder life, without a care.

Our thoughts drift like dandelions in flight,
Silly wishes spill under soft twilight.
And though night creeps in, it carries our cheer,
As we plot for more mischief when summer is here.

Starlit Echoes from Distant Shores

As twilight paints the fields with cheer,
The crickets chirp, a raucous leer.
Old Bob's hat is stuck on high,
He swears it's just a bird that flies.

The ice cream truck's a beacon bright,
With kids in chaos, what a sight!
While ducks play chess with swans mentee,
Who knew that life could be so free?

A cat struts by with utmost pride,
Wearing shades, he's on a ride.
He tips his hat to passing cars,
While dreaming of those candy bars.

We toast with soda, fizzy fun,
As laughter sparkles, one by one.
The stars above begin to twirl,
In this mad world, we spin and whirl.

Rhapsody of the Fading Light

The day bows down, it starts to purr,
While fireflies dance, what a blur!
Old Joe's shorts, a sight to see,
He claims they're fashion, oh so free!

The sun drops down, the moon wakes up,
And kids start racing, like a pup.
They trip on roots, they laugh, they squeal,
While mom sips tea, oh, how ideal!

In dodgy games of tag, they run,
Heads collide with luckless fun.
A watermelon's on the loose,
And Billy claims it's just a moose!

With lazy grins, we sit and gloat,
Over tales of Jerry's silly goat.
As dusk embraces all our dreams,
Life's wild antics burst at the seams.

The Dance of Fireflies

The twinkling lights begin to play,
Like tiny stars gone astray.
A glowworm wishes to join the crowd,
But trip on grass? Oh, there he bowed!

With laughter sprouting like a vine,
The kids' antics in line are divine.
They chase the flickers, show their might,
While grandpa snores, it's quite a sight!

The dance unfolds, a surreal show,
As laughter echoes, high and low.
A frog leaps in with an awkward croak,
While dad roasts marshmallows, woeful smoke!

The night gives way to funny tales,
Of pirate cats and grand whale trails.
And as the fireflies tire their dance,
We raise a toast to silly chance!

Sunkissed Echoes of the Day

With cheeks ablaze from sun's embrace,
We run around, a happy race.
A sack of chips, it's all a mess,
A picnic feast, we'd never guess!

The dog's in charge, he steals the fries,
While giggling kids all roll their eyes.
A frisbee flips, it meets a tree,
And down it falls, hilariously!

We splash in pools with great delight,
As cannonballs create a sight.
But splashes fly, and so do pants,
While grandma giggles at the dance.

The sunset blushes, a glowing prank,
As friends gather near to share a tank.
The day winds down, oh how it fades,
With echoes of laughter, joy cascades!

Whispered Secrets Under Falling Stars

Under twinkling lights we conspire,
Gathering tales of wild desire.
Our laughter echoes, oh what a scene,
As squirrels debate who's the best cuisine.

Ice cream drips on our summer clothes,
Laughter erupts as the neighbor doze.
A cat steals chips, oh the sneaky thief,
We swear it's magic, not just belief.

Behind us, a frog plays the violin,
We dance like fools, let the fun begin!
With a splash from the pond, we yell with glee,
Summer evenings, what a sight to see!

Falling grasshoppers join in our cheer,
Twirling around, we have no fear.
In this moment, our youth we claim,
Chasing the sunset, life is a game.

Ember Glow

The fire crackles, stories unfold,
A marshmallow gourmet, ginger, and bold.
The shadows dance as we roast away,
Who knew burnt snacks could spark such play?

A game of charades, what can we be?
An epic showdown with a bumblebee.
Between us, a chihuahua, dressed as a star,
Wagging his tail, he knows he's bizarre.

We fake our fear of the ghosts in the trees,
Around the flames, we giggle with ease.
With each tale we spin, the warmth takes hold,
Under the embers, our laughter is gold.

As the moon peeks out, we plot our next feat,
Like ninjas in slippers, we're light on our feet.
Summer nights whisk us away from our woes,
Carving memories, that's how it goes.

Frosted Hues of a Summer Ending

Leaves start to change, but we still play,
Ah, the last pool party, hip hip hooray!
With floats shaped like flamingos and pizza too,
Who knew swimming could be quite so goo?

We wade through the water with candy on hand,
Till a seagull swoops down, it's a wobbly stand.
Squeals of delight as we splash and we dive,
Wishing this twilight would always revive.

But soon comes the sunset, painting the skies,
We dodge the ice cream truck—what a surprise!
"Last scoop of summer!" the driver declares,
But we're too busy plucking off our hair.

With summer fading, we find the last zests,
Catching fireflies in our outlandish vests.
As the night whispers secrets, we chuckle and sigh,
Promising next summer we'll reach for the sky.

Sighs of the Solstice

The longest day fills our hearts with elation,
Under a sky of swirling rotation.
Jumping on trampolines, we bounce with cheer,
While planning the pranks that are drawing near.

A lemonade stand run by ducks in disguise,
They quack in protest, oh, what a surprise!
With giggles and splashes, we slip in the fun,
Until we realize, our year has begun.

Toward dusk, we create shadow puppets anew,
A dragon, a knight, and a girl in a shoe.
Chasing the stars in our glittery shoes,
We make up the rules, it's our game to choose.

As crickets sing songs that we wish would not end,
We plot silly dances, our bodies will bend.
Time moves too fast, but our laughter can flow,
In the moments of summer, we refuse to go slow.

Blush of the Evening

The sun slips down, a playful thief,
A sky like candy, can't help but grieve.
Squirrels in shades of orange so bright,
Chasing their tails, what a silly sight.

In the distance, children laugh and cheer,
Ice cream cones melting, sticky but dear.
A dog in sunglasses takes a long walk,
Wearing a hat, he starts to talk.

The fireflies dance, a tiny parade,
Buzzing with glee in this twilight shade.
I trip on a root, now I'm in a spin,
Just a hilarious evening, where to begin?

The stars peek out, a twinkling show,
And there's that raccoon, dressed for a pro.
He snatches my snack, it's all just for fun,
As the blush of the night has truly begun.

Elysium of Dusk

The clouds gather round in a giggly mood,
Swirling and twisting, not much is good.
A bird attempts a karaoke song,
But all the other birds just sing along!

A girl in a hammock swings with a grin,
Her cat on a diet, but not on a whim.
He jumps for a bug, oh what a mistake,
Now he's stuck in the tree, for heaven's sake!

Flip-flops on feet, what a silly clatter,
As friends throw popcorn, a comedic matter.
Laughter erupts as someone shouts,
"I'm not a seagull, just watch me pout!"

The horizon blushes, a comic delight,
While a deer photobombs, just to ignite.
And as we all gather, we giggle and cheer,
In this playful dusk, we hold close what's dear.

Wanderlust in the Twilight

At the edge of town where the kids race bikes,
A frog on a mission, but wishes for likes.
He leaps with a flair, jumps into a lake,
Plonks down with a splash, oh what a mistake!

A cat with sunglasses lounges and snores,
While a raccoon dances, checking 'what's yours.'
Birds try to hula, with style, if you please,
But end up all tangled, like spaghetti trees.

Lemonade spills as someone fools 'round,
The sugar ants joins, it's a sugary mound.
A kite in the sky gets stuck in a tree,
While our laughter rings out, so wild and so free.

Twilight arrives with a wink and a chuckle,
A firefly parade, and oh, what a bustle!
With dreams in our hearts, we adventure anew,
In this laughter-filled dusk, where the wild spirits flew.

Flutters of Fireflies

The evening creeps in, a shy little mouse,
While poppies gossip with a bright garden spouse.
Fireflies twinkle like laughter so bright,
As mosquitoes practice their dance in mid-flight.

Someone just fell in the grass with a thud,
Their soda spills out, oh what a big flood!
A dog runs by, wearing a silly hat,
Chasing those bugs, oh look at that!

Kids sharing stories in giggles of glee,
About their brave hero, a clumsy old bee.
He tried to impress all the flowers and trees,
But landed in yogurt, oh what a tease!

As stars explode like confetti in air,
We laugh till we snort, without any care.
In the glow of the night, with friends here to stay,
We cherish these flutters, as shadows play.

What the Light Remembers

A glow that winks like stars on toast,
They dance with shadows, they love to boast.
Jellybeans tumble from clouds above,
Fluttering dreams wrapped in a hug.

We chase the twilight, like kids on a spree,
Trading our worries for cups of sweet tea.
The cats serenade while we hum along,
In this goofy realm, there's no room for wrong.

Naps and laughs, all tangled in gold,
Stories of mishaps hilariously told.
Winks from the sun, like it's in on the joke,
Life's a comic strip, as we gently poke.

So let the lamp flicker, let the antics flow,
In the light's memory, we steal the show.
With a wink and a grin, we'll dance 'til it's late,
For in this warm glow, we create our fate.

Tides of Warmth and Mystery

The breeze tickles noses, and why not, eyes?
Giggling to stars dressed in upcycled ties.
We ride on marbles of laughter at play,
Sandy toes giggling all the way.

The ice cream's melting, but so is the dawn,
Now we're painting rainbows on breakfast's lawn.
Confetti of petals twist through the air,
Who needs a plan? We'll just wing it, I swear!

Sneakers in puddles, a splash and a shout,
Kites in the treetops, we laugh and we pout.
With giggles like bubbles in the wild wind's sway,
We steal little moments, come what may.

The world, oh how silly, wrapped in this glow,
Where time turns elastic, and joy's on show.
As dusk paints the sky, a mischievous friend,
We'll ride on this giggle 'til the very end.

Eden's Last Light

In a garden where laughter floats like the breeze,
The fruit's singing songs, rustling leaves with ease.
We wear flower crowns and giggle with glee,
As ants throw a party, just under a tree.

Fireflies blink, like they're trying to text,
While watermelon slices play tag, quite perplexed.
The sun's blurry face is yawning out loud,
While we get tangled among the crowd.

A frog croaks a tune; it might be a hit,
Funny how grass thinks it's softer to sit.
The time feels elastic as we spin and sway,
With silly old faces that lead us astray.

The angels above laugh with each nighttime cheer,
Each twinkle a wink, wrapped in warmth and cheer.
So let's gather the giggles as the day takes flight,
In an Eden so silly, under the last light.

Butterflies in the Last Glow

The butterflies flap in a peculiar dance,
Wearing tiny hats, oh what a chance!
We skip near the daisies, pretending to fly,
With giggles and doodles, under twilight sky.

Jars filled with wishes tossed into the breeze,
The crickets all chuckle, floating like leaves.
We've bet on this magic, what a wild ride,
While the stars play peekaboo from the riverside.

Socks mismatched, like our thoughts in a whirl,
Lemonade laughter with a twist and a swirl.
Each breath is a hiccup of hope and delight,
In a meadow where everything feels just right.

With shadows growing, we hide from the night,
Dreaming of pancakes and whimsical flight.
As the glow dims softer, we grab hold of fun,
With kisses to twilight, our laughter still spun.

Celestial Caresses at Sundown

The sun dips low, a flaming ball,
Kids chase fireflies, watch them fall.
Grandpa's stories, all a bit tall,
Laughter erupts, echoes through the hall.

Ice cream drips down sticky hands,
As ants form lines in little bands.
Jokes are told in funny strands,
While tiny feet make wiggle plans.

A soft breeze giggles through the trees,
Whispers of secrets in the leaves.
Tickling toes and giddy wheezes,
As stars appear like sparkling fees.

With twilight's grin, it's time for play,
Four-legged friends join in the fray.
In this joyful dance, we sway,
Until the night takes the light away.

Midsummer's Gentle Whispers

The clouds wear pajamas, fluffy and white,
While squirrels debate what's wrong or right.
In the garden, the flowers delight,
With bees putting on a sugar-fueled flight.

A cooler breeze tickles our skin,
As popsicles melt, no chance to win.
Kids snicker over a silly spin,
While parents just try to keep their chin.

The moon peeks out, a big old grin,
Two cats on the fence, each seeking kin.
The night is young; let the games begin,
As laughter rings, it's pure din.

From twilight's charm to stars so bright,
Day turns to mischief, what a sight!
In this sweet chaos, everything's right,
We dance with joy until morning light.

The Lure of Twilight's Charm

The sun bows down, with flair and fawn,
Children's giggles greet the dawn.
On golden grass, a lively lawn,
Where dreams and chuckles easily spawn.

Fireworks in bellies, the candy parade,
Bikes race ahead, no need for trade.
In this fun chaos, childhood's made,
With silly antics that never fade.

The crickets sing, a quirky tune,
While shadows elongate beneath the moon.
We gather close, as laughter's our boon,
Sharing tales that make hearts swoon.

As dusk wraps us in its playful clutch,
Every sigh is a happy touch.
With whispers of fun, oh so much,
In this twilight, we feel the rush.

Fabric of the Evening Sky

Sweaters in summer? A curious twist,
With stars overhead, how could we miss?
Twinkle lights blink, a cosmic kiss,
While cupcakes dance on a frosty list.

Moonbeams jest, all silvery-sweet,
As toddlers parade with sticky feet.
In this warm glow, we can't retreat,
From giggles and wishes, life's little treat.

As shadows play games, we join the fun,
Count shooting stars, let the night run.
Joyful shouts, we've all been spun,
Embraced by the sky, we are one.

When laughter fades with the morning's light,
We'll remember this fun, our hearts so bright.
In the fabric of the sky, pure delight,
Summer whispers, holding us tight.

www.ingramcontent.com/pod-product-compliance
Lightning Source LLC
Chambersburg PA
CBHW070321120526
44590CB00017B/2776